FACT ATTACK

SPECTACULAR SPACE

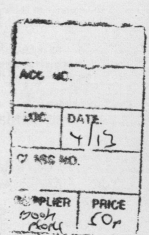

ACC NC.		
LOC.	DATE 4/13	
C MSS NO.		
SUPPLIER mooh morl	PRICE 50p	

IAN LOCKE

MACMILLAN CHILDREN'S BOOKS

First published 1999 by Macmillan Children's Books

This edition published 2012 by Macmillan Children's Books
a division of Macmillan Publishers Limited
20 New Wharf Road, London N1 9RR
Basingstoke and Oxford
Associated companies throughout the world
www.panmacmillan.com

ISBN 978-1-4472-2440-2

135798642

A CIP catalogue record for this book is available from
the British Library.

Printed and bound by CPI Group (UK) Ltd, Croydon CR0 4YY

DID YOU KNOW THAT . . .

 The medical kit issued to the astronauts on the American space station Skylab included pills for travel sickness!

 Pictures of a spiral around a huge black hole were received from the Hubble space telescope on May 26 1994. The black hole was said to be as dense as three billion suns!

 During a May night in 1994, Uganda was hit by at least 863 lumps of meteorite. Luckily, only one boy was injured and a banana tree broke the fall of the lump that hit him.

 The tiny neutron star, left over when a star collapses, is so heavy that a piece the size of a pinhead would weigh as much as a supertanker.

1

The longest recorded solar eclipse was recorded on January 15 2010. It lasted 11 minutes, 7.8 seconds.

 The US comic duo Abbott and Costello starred in *Abbott and Costello Go To Mars*. But oddly enough, the planet they go to in the film is Venus!

 Major Titov of the USSR is the youngest person so far to have gone into space, at the age of 25 years and 329 days.

 The first space shuttle was originally named the OV (Orbiter Vehicle) 101. It was later named the Enterprise and was tested in August 1977 over California.

A black and white teddy bear, Mishka, went into space aboard the Soviet Salyut 6 in 1979. Mishka was the first teddy bear to orbit the earth.

 Pierre Gassendi observed the transit of the planet Mercury on November 7 1631. This was the first time the transit of a planet had been observed and recorded.

 The Hubble space telescope was launched on April 24 1990.

 The three words spoken at the launch of the first US manned rocket, on May 5 1961, were not what you might think. They were: "Ignition . . . Mainstage . . . Lift-off."

Major Virgil Grissom of the USA became the first man to fly in space twice when he took off from Cape Kennedy in 1964.

 Space is a funny environment. If an average person stays weightless in space for 4.5 months they will lose about 12 per cent or one eighth of their pelvic bone. In time, fluid will also get into the brain, making the head foggy, so that it becomes impossible to think straight. At the moment, if someone travelled to Mars, the loss of calcium in their bones would be so great that by the time they arrived they would only be able to crawl!

 Phobos, the Soviet probe orbiting Mars, disappeared in 1989. It was claimed it had been intercepted by Martians!

It is estimated that the sun weighs 330,000 times as much as the earth.

 The first docking of one space vehicle with another was the docking of the Gemini-Titan VII rocket with the GT-VI, both American spacecraft.

 The planet Neptune was first found in 1795, but at the time it was thought to be just another star. It was re-discovered in 1846.

 In April 1968 an agreement was signed by many countries, including Britain, the USA and the then Soviet Union, to rescue any astronauts in trouble.

When astronauts shave in space they use razors with a vacuum attachment so that the bristles do not float about in the capsule.

 On the planet Mercury, a day is two-thirds the length of a year. It takes just under 88 days for the planet to revolve around the sun and 58.6 days for it to revolve around its own axis.

 Nearly a quarter of the world's population watched American astronaut Neil Armstrong take the first human step on the moon on July 20 1969. At first, Mission Control were frightened that he would sink into the moon-dust, but they needn't have worried. The lack of gravity meant that his footsteps were only three millimetres deep and that his backpack, which had weighed 227 kg back on Earth, weighed only 45 kg on the moon!

An asteroid weighing half a million tons passed 485,000 miles from the earth on October 30 1937.

 The toilet for the space shuttle Endeavour cost £19.5 million to build.

 Europa, Jupiter's moon, is thought to have a sea below its surface.

 When the Russians launched the first spacecraft, the Sputnik (or "Fellow Traveller"), on October 4 1957, it was called a "pathetic bubble" in the United States.

 The features of the moon of planet Uranus are all named after characters from Shakespeare's plays.

In 1993 the autographed flight instructions for the first man in space, Yuri Gagarin, were sold in New York for $70,000.

 Light travels at a speed of nearly 10 billion kilometres a year.

 The craters on the planet Mercury are named after great artists, musicians and writers, including Van Gogh, Matisse, Beethoven, Wagner and Milton.

 The fastest man-made vehicle is the Ulysses space probe which travels at 27.4 miles per second.

On their first trip to the moon, the Americans left a tribute to the astronauts who died in Apollo 1 and to the two Soviet cosmonauts Yuri Gagarin and Vladimir Komarov. They also left a golden olive branch to symbolize peace.

 Very few people have had the chance to see an eclipse as clearly as those who once travelled on Concorde. Passengers aboard the supersonic plane were able to watch a total eclipse of the sun for one hour and 14 minutes, when flying from Toulouse in France to Chad, Africa.

 Boiling and freezing take place at the same temperature in space.

In 1054, on July 5, a minor star exploded into a supernova which was visible by day for 23 days and by night for 633 nights. This then formed the Crab nebula, which is now an especially strong source of radio waves and X-rays.

 In 1456 Pope Calixtus III declared that Halley's comet was an agent of the Devil and excommunicated it!

 Small craters on Venus are named after famous women including Florence Nightingale.

 Ulugh Beg made the first catalogue of stars in 1018. His calculations about the movements of the planets Venus and Mars were very accurate – only 5 and 7 seconds different from 20th-century figures.

Bonnie Dunbar simply reached out and caught a satellite from the space shuttle Columbia in January 1990. It was the largest orbiting satellite to be recovered.

 Some important dates in space:

1957. The first satellite (Sputnik) is launched by Russia.

1959. Manned rockets are proposed in the USA.

1960 (May). A dummy astronaut is launched by the Russians.

1961 (April). Yuri Gagarin of Russia becomes the first man in space.

1961 (May). Alan Shepard becomes the first American in space.

1962 (July). The first satellite TV is introduced.

1965. Two Soviet cosmonauts walk in space.

1969 (July). The first men land on the moon.

1970. The first Chinese satellite is launched.

1970. The first Japanese satellite is launched.

1971 (December). The first craft lands on Mars.

1972 (July). The first craft lands on Venus.

1976. The first US spacecraft lands on Mars and takes photos.

1990 (April). The Hubble space telescope is launched.

1997 (July). The Mars Pathfinder lands.

 The most dramatic of space ventures took place in 1970. On April 13, Mission Control in Houston, USA, lost communication with Apollo 13 for two seconds. No one noticed. But just after 9.00 that day, the three astronauts noticed a yellow alarm flash and a shudder moved through the craft. An explosion had taken place in one of the fuel tanks and two fuel cells were out. Astronaut Jim Swigert signalled back to Earth with the words

"Houston, we have a problem". The spacecraft began to wobble and the planned moon landing was quickly abandoned. Houston realized that the craft was losing power and the oxygen supply was beginning to fall. Apollo 13 was over 300,000 miles from Earth. After moving into the lunar module, the astronauts were able to fire the engine in an attempt to return to Earth. For two tense days, the attention of the world was on the three men. They went without sleep, and put together a way of keeping oxygen in the cold module. Eventually, they were able to fire the engine for re-entry to the earth's atmosphere. To everyone's relief, they made it.

 A red dwarf star does exist. It has a temperature of 2,226°C, but is still cooler than a white dwarf star.

When the US Apollo X re-entered the earth's atmosphere in 1969, it was travelling at 24,790.8 miles an hour – faster than man had ever flown before.

 On July 31 1992, the US space shuttle Atlantis launched a carrier containing bacteria and DNA material into space.

 The chimps that the Americans sent into space have their own retirement home and park in California.

 The planet Mercury has huge curving cliffs known as "rupes".

 In 1980 it was found that cosmonauts Leonid Popov and Valery Ryumin had grown three centimetres during their record 185-day space flight.

A memorial was unveiled in July 1991 at the Kennedy Space Center, USA, for the fifteen astronauts who died "believing the conquest of space is worth the risk of life".

 In 1968, the British member of parliament Tony Benn said Britain was to give up a lot of its space research. He said he could see "no future in satellites".

 When man first landed on the moon, the controllers in Houston space centre were locked in so no one could disturb them!

 In 2011, the rubber ears of Mr Spock of *Star Trek* were sold for an estimated £700 at auction.

 The range of temperature for a Martian day runs from -30 to -86°C.

A meteor, believed to be a relic from near the time of creation, hit the earth's atmosphere in June 1998. It was reported as a UFO by people from Devon to North Wales.

 Many clocks show the position of the stars. They are called astronomical clocks. The magnificent clock at Beauvais Cathedral, France, took three years to complete. It was finished in 1868.

 The military base of Plesetsk, Russia, is used for space launches. A few years ago it ran out of money and had its electricity cut off!

 Twelve people at Mission Control, Houston, had to give the go-ahead for the moon landing in 1969. Everyone said "Go". If someone had said "No go", then man would not have gone on to land on the moon.

A colour picture of the whole universe can now be put together by images taken from a radio telescope. It's a pretty picture because the colours change as the amount of radiation in the universe changes. The red parts show the centre of the universe.

 Lumps of odd rock and debris, known as asteroids, collect around the larger planets. Those near Jupiter travel at up to 60,000 miles an hour.

 The first asteroid was discovered by Italian Giuseppe Piazzi of the observatory in Palermo, Sicily, on January 1 1801.

 Pluto is 5,914 million kilometres from the sun.

These are some of the abbreviations which you need to know in space:

PDI – Power Descent Initiation (you can land).

TLI – Translunar Injection (go for the moon).

LM – Lunar Module.

ICBM – Intercontinental Ballistic Missile.

NASA – The National Aeronautics and Space Administration.

 The words "The eagle has landed" were spoken on the moon in July 1969. The Eagle was the name of the small craft that had landed on the moon.

When the Pioneer space probe sent signals back to Earth on its mission to Jupiter, it took 46 minutes for the information to arrive at the Ames Research Centre in California, USA. When the probe reached Saturn, the signals took 173 minutes to arrive. The 26 kg craft was the first man-made object to escape the solar system. It will take another 36,500 years for it to get close to the nearest red dwarf star – Ross 248. Even then, the tiny red dwarf will be 3.3 light years away!

 An explosion on the sun, called a blinker, is equivalent to the explosion of 100 tons of dynamite.

 A moon rocket has the same amount of power as 543 jet fighters.

There are up to 45,000 asteroids between Mars and Jupiter. Many are now numbered and given names, including Hilda, Marilyn and Sabrina. No. 2309 is named after Mr Spock of *Star Trek*!

 The planet Neptune and its moon were discovered by the English brewer and part-time stargazer William Lassell, in 1846.

 A sunquake has enough energy to power the USA for 20 years. The average sunquake is 10,000 times as strong as the huge San Francisco earthquake of 1906.

When Vietnam was at war with America in the 1960s, the government of North Vietnam were so worried about the Americans being the first to land on the moon that in 1969 they told the Vietnamese that it was the Russians who had landed.

 Captain Bruce McCandless of the USA became the first person to enter space without life-support lines and the first to move in a void when he stepped out of his capsule on February 7 1984.

 In 1930, an American, Karl Jansky, was asked to find out why there was so much hiss on the new car radios. When he came back to the people at the Bell telephone company in America, his answer was astounding. The noise, he said, came from the Milky Way! The whole galaxy was alive with radiation which was picked up as sound, causing the pops, hiss and crackle on the radio.

On November 3 1957, the Soviet dog Leika became the first animal in space. Two mice were the next animals in space. They were sent up in a US rocket on December 13 1958.

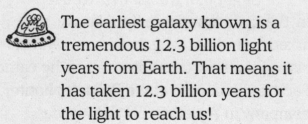 David Ashford of Britain tested a model of his own spaceplane, the Ascender, in May 1998. It worked.

The earliest galaxy known is a tremendous 12.3 billion light years from Earth. That means it has taken 12.3 billion years for the light to reach us!

One of the messages sent into space on the Voyager 2 craft was in Latin, the language of Ancient Rome. It said, "Greetings to you, wherever you are; we have good will towards you and bring peace across space." The Chinese message was a bit different: "Hope everyone's well. We are thinking about you all. Please come here to visit us when you have time." So, when aliens do turn up on your doorstep, remember, they were invited!

 Before the 16th century, astrophysicists thought that the planets would eventually spiral into the sun.

 1,300 Earths can fit into the planet Jupiter.

 The thrust of a rocket sent into space is a massive 349,000 kg – equal to thousands of super hot-rod cars being revved up at the same time.

Virgil Grissom, the US astronaut, had a lucky escape in July 1961, when his capsule sank after it made a parachute landing in the Atlantic Ocean. As water began to pour in through the escape hatch, he had to swim for his life. He was picked up by a helicopter a few minutes later.

 In 2011 Sir Richard Branson announced that Virgin Galactic would shortly pioneer trips into space for the public, aboard their specially designed spacecraft. The company is now taking bookings – tickets currently cost $200,000.

 America was given a holiday to celebrate man's first landing on the moon.

The world's largest meteorite was discovered on a farm in South Africa. Known as the Hoba West, it weighs a terrific 54.4 tonnes and measures 2.73 metres by 2.43 metres – even after one million years out in the sun and rain!

 The American Skylab space station went into space in 1973. It was 15 metres long and 7 metres wide – about the size of a two-bedroom house. There was a kitchen and a workshop on board. It had to be shielded from the sun and, on the side in shadow, from the cold. Outside, the temperature could reach 163°C. If unprotected, the interior temperature could have reached 88°C, boiling the people inside!

 A flight of the US space shuttle was once held up by a woodpecker, who decided that the nose cone would be a suitable object to peck. The dozy bird was eventually persuaded to go away.

The moon is thought to have separated from the earth about 3,000 million years ago.

 When Apollo 11 landed the first men on the moon, the American President, Nixon, said that it had been "the greatest week in history since the Creation".

 A comet which appeared over Italy in 1347 was described as a black star and was said to foretell doom. The Black Death arrived in Europe within months.

 In 1572, when aged 26, Tycho Brahe, the Danish astronomer, discovered a new star. This proved that there had been a change in the heavens. He also saw a supernova, later named Tycho's star.

In 1967, an Action Man astronaut was on sale in toyshops. He had his own space capsule.

 The US space organization, NASA, played "Space Invaders" during the summer of 1998. This was part of the Near Earth Object programme, aimed at trying to prevent a rogue lump of junk or rock hitting the earth.

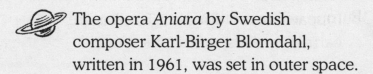 The opera *Aniara* by Swedish composer Karl-Birger Blomdahl, written in 1961, was set in outer space.

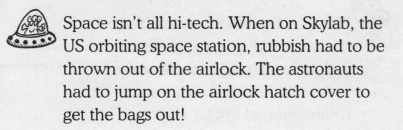 Space isn't all hi-tech. When on Skylab, the US orbiting space station, rubbish had to be thrown out of the airlock. The astronauts had to jump on the airlock hatch cover to get the bags out!

Helen Sharman, the first British astronaut, was 27 when she took off from Russia in the Soyuz TM 12 on May 19 1991. She was subsidized by a Moscow bank. The cost of her trip was said to be £5 million.

 A rocket has to travel at over 17,450 miles an hour to leave the earth's atmosphere and not be dragged back by gravity.

 In space, bread dries out. Tortillas are carried on the space shuttle instead.

 Britain's largest telescope, the 20-centimetre Great Equatorial Refractor telescope, was installed at the Old Royal Observatory, Greenwich, in 1893.

The five Tracy sons in the famous TV series *Thunderbirds*, made by Gerry Anderson in the 1960s, were all named after real US astronauts.

 The nearest star to the sun is called Proxima Centauri. It is a mere 34 billion kilometres away!

 The great German astronomer Johannes Kepler was 38 when he established two of the principles of astronomy: that planets travel round the sun in elliptical orbits, and that they do not travel at a constant speed.

 During the second American Skylab mission in 1978, all three US astronauts were very ill with motion sickness.

The space shuttle reaches a height of 43 kilometres above the earth in only two minutes!

 The Russians sent all sorts of living things into space in the 1960s – plants, insects, frogs, rabbits, guinea pigs and dogs.

 On the Apollo 8 mission of 1968, the US astronauts James Lovell, Frank Borman and William Anders were the first people to see the dark side of the moon.

 There are 1,400 switches and circuit breakers in the cockpit of the US space shuttle.

 The year on the moon (the lunar year) is 29.25 days shorter than the year on the sun (the solar year).

It may seem incredible, but iron on the moon does not rust. Samples of the iron brought back by both the American and Russian expeditions have remained rust-free for years.

 In 1997 a survey in the USA found that many Americans believed that the first moon landing of 1969 was faked by NASA.

 In the 1990s there were scares about an asteroid hitting the earth early in the next century. NASA had a look and decided that the probability of an impact was zero. So there!

 It takes 8 minutes and 38 seconds for the sun's rays to reach the earth, so at the moment we look at it, it is not actually where we see it, but has travelled a bit relative to us.

The US spacecraft Mariner 4 became the first to fly past Mars on July 14 1965. It sent back 22 close-up photos of the red planet, but unfortunately they were in black and white!

In 1854 a meteorite weighing over 5 tonnes was found at Cronbourne in Victoria, Australia.

The beauty of the Milky Way was confirmed when the Royal Academy, London, displayed a huge photo of the galaxy by Franklin Adams. It was made on 200 glass plate negatives and showed about 55 million stars!

A full moon is nine times brighter than a half moon.

A stamp of 1991, produced in the USA, included a hologram of an orbiting space station and space shuttle.

 On January 7 1610, Galileo of Italy became the first to see the three moons of Jupiter. His work was considered heresy by the Church, since he supported the idea that the planets move around the sun. As a result he was confined to his home from 1633 to 1641, after a trial by the Inquisition of the Catholic Church.

 The force of meteor explosions can be huge. There was a 2-kiloton blast above the Pacific on October 1 1990 as a meteor bounced off the earth's atmosphere. From 1974 to 1994, US satellites picked up at least three explosions above Britain.

Julius Caesar, the Roman leader, believed comets indicated the death of great people.

 Greenwich observatory was established in 1676.

 The British actor Sir Alec Guinness was given 2.25 per cent of the profits of the *Star Wars* films as part of his agreement to appear in them. So far, *Star Wars* alone, the first of the three films, has made over $775 million!

 In the Somali language, a satellite is "a star that failed to reach Heaven".

 After the 1986 shuttle disaster in the USA, there were 400 design changes made for the new shuttle, the Discovery.

Water was found on the moon by the US lunar prospector probe in March 1998. There was enough water there to support up to 10,000 two-person households for over 100 years!

 Halley discovered the comet named after him in 1682, confirming that it had appeared in 1607 and 1531. He did not live long enough to see it again in 1757.

 The temperature of Pluto is approximately -220°C.

 French physicist Armand Fizeau discovered the speed of light in 1849. It is about 300,000 kilometres an hour.

On February 3 1993, Russian scientists demonstrated the reflection of the sun's rays using a 20-metre parachute-shaped mirror from 340 kilometres above the earth. The mirror was made from Kevlar (a thin, tough fabric), covered with a thin layer of aluminium. The mirror was unfurled on the Progress craft sent from Mir, and a strip of land about 7 kilometres wide was lit up in central Europe.

In 1687 the astronomer Edmund Halley paid for Newton's work on the laws of gravity to be published.

Lieutenant James Cook (later Captain Cook) was sent to Tahiti in 1768 to set up an observatory so that the planet Venus's movement across the sun could be seen.

In 1781 William Herschel discovered the planet Uranus when using a home-made telescope in his garden in Bath. It was the first new planet to be discovered for 4,000 years, since Babylonian prehistory.

 A Dr Slipper discovered the ninth and most distant planet in our solar system, the dwarf planet Pluto, on March 13 1930 at the Lowell Observatory, USA.

 As the Eagle was coming in to land on the moon for the first time ever, astronauts Neil Armstrong and Buzz Aldrin found that their computer had failed. They were guided down by speaking to the Houston space centre.

 The first TV pictures of the earth were taken by the Explorer VI, a US spacecraft, in September 1959.

On January 7 1990 the satellite Voyager took the first pictures of the earth and its neighbouring planets from outside the solar system.

 The first name for a telescope was a "looker".

 When a massive star collapses and explodes, it is called a supernova. A huge amount of energy is released when this happens. In recorded human history only two supernovas are known of. One was seen in 1604 and another on February 23 1987, by a 30-year-old Canadian, Ian Skelton. He was using an old telescope at the mountain observatory of Las Campanas, Chile, when he photographed the supernova.

The first pictures of the rivers and channel-like features on the surface of Mars were sent back to Earth by the US spacecraft Mariner 9 on November 24 1971.

 In May 1991 the first recorded meteorite to fall in Britain for 26 years landed in the back garden of a house in the village of Glatton near Peterborough.

 Just before the first manned space flight, the two cosmonauts, Gagarin and Tîtov, appeared before the capsule in spacesuits and helmets. They clashed helmets as they sought to kiss each other in the traditional good luck greeting.

Looking at stars became popular in France in the 17th century. Some people thought themselves grand to have a telescope. A man called Periese kept a telescope at home and had big parties so people could come and look at the stars.

 The spacesuit worn by the first man on the moon, Neil Armstrong, had six layers. It was extremely light.

 There are 400 billion stars in the Milky Way.

 The countdown "Three, two, one, lift-off" was first used in the 1929 German film *The Woman in the Moon* by Fritz Lang. The effects were so real that the German dictator, Hitler, later ordered that all plans and models of the rockets used in the film should be destroyed and that the film itself should be banned.

To test how well their hearts work, astronauts have to lie head down on a very sloping table for 25 minutes.

 Rock music connected with space became very popular in the 1960s and 1970s. Among the best-known bands with a space theme were Pink Floyd. Their songs include:
1. 'The Great Gig in the Sky'
2. 'Set the Controls to the Heart of the Sun'
3. 'Astronomy Domine'
4. 'Point Me at the Sky'
5. 'Eclipse'
6. 'Dark Side of the Moon'
7. 'Interstellar Overdrive'

 In June 1983, Valentina Tereshkova of Russia became the first woman in space.

A Mars meteorite was put up for sale by American Robert Haag for £1.3 million in 1992. He is the only full-time meteorite hunter in the world.

 On August 21 1995, NASA's expensive Mars Observer vanished as it approached Mars.

 The first person recorded as having been injured by a meteorite was Mrs Ann Hodges of Sylacauga in Alabama, USA, on November 30 1954. A 4 kg meteorite crashed through the roof of her house and hit her on the arm and bruised her hip.

 The Sojourner Rover, sent out by the US Mars Pathfinder on July 4 1997, became the first vehicle to be used on the surface of another planet.

The word meteor comes from an Ancient Greek word that means "things in the air".

 The American John Glenn's first space flight, which took place on February 20 1962, lasted 4 hours and 56 minutes. He went into the capsule three hours before he took off and was in the capsule for only 12 hours in total.

 Only five or six of the 500 or so meteorites which fall on the earth each year are found.

 Shooting stars are really meteorites burning up in the earth's atmosphere.

 A star which disappeared around the same time as the dinosaurs was discovered in 1994.

A huge bubble of gas was thrown from the sun towards the earth in January 1997. Material explodes from the sun almost every day, but only rarely towards the earth.

 After the assassination of President John Kennedy of the USA on November 22 1963, the US space launch station, Cape Canaveral in Florida, was renamed Cape Kennedy.

 The Galileo spacecraft, costing £500 million, was launched from the space shuttle Atlantis in 1989.

 Aida, a huge asteroid measuring 4.6 metres wide, 5.5 metres deep and 56 kilometres long, was found by the spacecraft Galileo in 1994. It was even big enough to have its own moon, which was nearly 2 kilometres wide and orbiting about 97 kilometres away.

A satellite weighing 23 kg with 400 million tiny copper needles, each 2 centimetres long and finer than a human hair, was put into orbit by the United States in May 1963. It was found to reflect radio waves.

 In 1994, a series of ads in British newspapers brought a message from Sister Marie Gabriel, predicting that the comet Shoemaker Levy would collide with Jupiter in July of that year and destroy the solar system. The comet did hit Jupiter, but the solar system is still here. It turned out that Sister Marie Gabriel was a Sophie Richmond, who lived in Cricklewood, London.

 The patron saint of astronauts is St Joseph of Cupertino.

On December 6 1993, Tom Akers set a new US record with a space walk of 22 hours, 50 minutes from the space shuttle Endeavour, beating the previous record by a minute. His co-astronaut, Kathy Thornton, set a new female record of 14 hours, 12 minutes.

 The Mars Polar Lander space mission of 1998 was unusual: on board was a CD-ROM with the names of one million children from all over the world.

 US astronaut Alan Shepard did some unique golf practice . . . on the moon. He used a 6-iron and drove a golf ball some 366 metres.

 The French space centre at Kourou in French Guiana, South America, launched its first scientific rocket Véronique in April 1968.

On a mission to Mars, people would have to be sheltered from four types of rays: cosmic rays, the rays of the Van Allen radiation belts, nuclear rays and giant solar flares. Their water – for washing and drinking – also has to be protected so it does not turn radioactive.

 In 1993, US astronaut Kathy Thornton, on the Endeavour space shuttle, was able to easily remove a twisted solar panel which would have weighed 180 kg on earth.

 It has been found that animals and people use their eyes more in space, instead of relying on the balance organs in their ears to know where they are.

 When Galileo used his early telescopes in the 17th century, the best he could do was magnify things by twenty.

By 2011, 55 women had flown in space. 45 were American, 3 Soviet/Russian, 2 Canadian, 2 Japanese, 1 French, 1 South Korean and 1 British – Helen Sharman.

 John Glenn, the first US astronaut, was also the first person to fly across the United States at supersonic speed.

 The early British astronomer John Flamsteed spent £2,000 of his own money on telescopes and other instruments in the 18th century so he could look at the stars. He worked for twelve years on a book which showed 20,000 of the stars he had seen.

 On his historic mission to the moon in 1969, Neil Armstrong's left glove carried a stitched-on list of tasks.

Tiny diamonds are believed to be in the dust clouds in space.

 When the American space station Skylab was being put into the Smithsonian Museum in Washington in 1974, it was found to be far too big. NASA obligingly cut it into four pieces so it could be reassembled indoors.

 Lord Posse of Parsonstown, Ireland, built a giant telescope on his Irish estate in 1843.

 US President Nixon gave his governors pieces of moon rock in December 1969. They had been brought back from the moon on Apollo 11.

There is now so much artificial light at night in cities that seeing the stars is close to impossible. All the big observatories for seeing stars are now well away from cities.

 An early job for the first man in space, Russian Yuri Gagarin, was making aircraft parts in a factory!

 An ancient legend in Cambodia says that during an eclipse of the moon, the moon is being eaten by a giant frog.

 The "terminator" is the line between the sunlit and dark parts of the moon.

 The 100th space walk took place on May 14 1992 when astronauts on the US space shuttle tested out the walks to be used for the building of the future space station, Freedom.

The first close encounter between a spacecraft and an asteroid happened in 1991 when the Galileo probe just missed an asteroid measuring 6.25 miles by 11 miles, between Mars and Jupiter.

 Freeze-dried chicken and pot roast were among the foods on the first manned US space flights.

 Helen Sharman, the first British person in space, once said that the most common question she was asked was how she went to the lavatory in space.

 A detailed map of the moon was drawn by the Italian priest Riccioli in 1651.

 Space vehicles and supersonic jets are made from the metal titanium. It is the world's strongest metal for its weight.

Sir Arthur C. Clarke, the leading British sci-fi writer and inventor of the communications satellite, obtained a top first class degree in Physics and Maths from King's College, London, after only two years instead of the usual three.

 The first probe sent to Venus by the West, launched on August 27 1962, was tracked from South Africa, Australia and California, USA.

 Here are the names of some of the spaceships which appear in films. The USS *Enterprise* in *Star Trek* is well known, but others include:

1. United Nations One – *First Men in the Moon* (1965)
2. Discovery – *2001, A Space Odyssey* (1968)
3. Dark Star – *Dark Star* (1974)
4. Millennium Falcon – *Star Wars* (1977)
5. Luna – *Destination Moon* (1950)
6. Nostromo – *Alien* (1980)

The enormous canyon *Valles Marineris* stretches nearly a third of the way round the planet Mars.

 It is reckoned that the force of the asteroid that made the huge crater in Arizona was equivalent to that of 800 atom bombs.

 Of the total weight of a rocket, only 1.8–3 per cent is usually the actual object or person put into space. The rest is used up and sent back to Earth or left as junk in space.

 The first man in space, Yuri Gagarin, was tiny. He was only 1.52 metres tall.

 British-born astronaut Michael Foale spent 145 days aboard the Russian space station Mir in 1997.

The sun is 27,000 light years from the centre of the galaxy.

 In 1961 the US Post Office introduced "speed mail" – messages sent by satellite. They were printed out on earth and delivered. E-mail has now replaced this system.

 Telstar 1, a satellite launched in July 1962, made international TV possible for the first time. It also made long-distance phone calls easier.

 One of the tests early astronauts had to undertake was to plunge their feet in ice-cold water, then spend two hours in a room at a temperature of 54°C.

Films about the moon and the planets have always been popular. Some of the odder films include:
1. *Catwomen of the Moon*
2. *Radar Men from the Moon*
3. *Mouse on the Moon*
4. *Gulliver's Travels Beyond the Moon*
5. *Girl in the Moon*

In 1803, a French physicist said that meteors (shooting stars) were imagined and that people made up stories about them.

The training pool for the space shuttle is so big that four space shuttles could fit in it.

Russian cosmonaut Tsibliev was filmed drinking long-life milk on the space station Mir in August 1997. It was part of a £280,000 Israeli TV commercial.

For some reason the first colour satellite TV pictures were mostly pink.

 We are still here . . . just. Satellites are not always perfect. In September 1983, the world could have been blown up by nuclear weapons. A Russian Cosmos satellite went wrong that day and sent a message to Earth saying that the United States had launched nuclear missiles which were on their way to Russia. A smart Russian soldier decided that the satellite had made a mistake and quickly told the authorities not to launch the Russian missiles. They agreed it was a fault. Phew!

 In 1565, when aged nineteen, the great Danish astronomer Tycho Brahe lost his nose in a fight. He then wore a false nose made of silver and gold which he stuck on with cement – a pot of which he always carried around with him, just in case. He was later given an island to work from by King Frederick II of Denmark.

The Mars Pathfinder expedition of 1997 discovered that ancient Mars had been wet and possibly able to support life.

 Working on a mission to Mars in the 1980s, the Russians conducted experiments in human hibernation for space travel.

 Anaxagorus, a Greek philosopher who died in 428 BC, was condemned for the weird idea he had that the sun was a molten rock measuring 100 miles across which glowed with super-heat, instead of a flat disc in the sky. Of course he was right – apart from the size.

Close to dawn on June 30 1908, a huge flash was seen in the sky and a loud bang was heard over the thick forests of the remote area of Tunguska, Siberia. Villagers up to two hundred miles away fled in terror. A number of people were badly burned or thrown through the air as a massive fireball hurtled to Earth. For some 40 miles from the centre of the event, the trees were blown down in patterns showing the direction of the blast. Scientists only reached the remote spot years later, in 1927. They found no tell-tale signs of a meteorite impact or a crater. The cause remains a mystery, though it is likely it was a comet which exploded just above the earth. The ice and dust would have left no visible evidence.

 One of the first things done by the second man in space, Major Titov of the Soviet Union, was to turn his radio on!

 58

During the 1950s and 1960s, one of the most common free gifts in cereal packets was a spaceship. As a boy, Prince Charles collected them.

 When cosmonaut Poliakoff of the then Soviet Union spent 15 months in space, it was found that being in space makes the heart slow down. This makes it impossible for a person to return to Earth without exercising while in space.

 The first observatory was established in Nuremberg in 1471. The astronomer who designed it saw Halley's comet the next year.

 Seen from space, the edge of the earth is blue and purple.

 When he wasn't otherwise busy, Galileo composed music for the lute.

The first nebula (constellation of stars), Andromeda, was recorded as early as 963 by the Arabian Al Sufi.

 On May 18 1998 the US space agency NASA decided to keep news of any earthbound asteroid a secret.

 In the 1980s it was found that cosmic dust lies at the bottom of the sea.

 The earth is surrounded by a ring of dust.

 While in space on the shuttle Columbia in October 1995, astronaut Lopez-Alegria logged onto the Internet.